HILDILID'S NIGHT

BY CHELI DURÁN RYAN
ILLUSTRATED BY ARNOLD LOBEL

COLLIER BOOKS
Division of Macmillan Publishing Co., Inc.
New York

High in the hills near Hexham
there lived an old woman named Hildilid.

She hated bats and owls and moles and voles

and moths and stars and shadows and sleep,
and even the moonlight, all because she hated the night.

"If only," said Hildilid to her old wolfhound,
"I could chase the night from Hexham,
  the sun would always shine on my hut.
  I do not know why no one has thought
  of chasing away the night before."

  Hildilid cut a broom from twigs
  to sweep the night out of her hut
  and over the hills of Hexham.

  She swept and scrubbed and scoured and whisked,
  but whenever she looked out of her window,
  the night was still there,
  like dust behind rafters.

Hildilid pulled out her needle and sewed sackcloth
into a strong sack to see if she could fill it with the night
and empty it beyond the hills of Hexham.

She wadded and padded and pushed and stuffed,
and she even sneaked up on the shadows,
but she could not cram all the night into a sack.

Hildilid dragged her heaviest caldron to the fire
so she could boil away the night.
She ladled it, stirred it, simmered it,
bubbled it, tasted it, and burned it,
but she could not boil away the night.

Hildilid gathered vines to tie the night up
into a neat bundle.
"Perhaps someone will buy it in the market," she thought.
But she could not tie up the night.

Hildilid sheared the night
like a sheep,
but all that dropped
from the sky
was a little cloud.

She tossed the night to her old wolfhound
stretched on the rushes,
but he could not wolf down the night.

She tucked the night into her straw bed,
but it jumped out.

She ducked the night in the well behind her hovel,
but it bobbed up.

She singed the night with a candle,
but it skipped outside.

Hildilid sang it lullabies,

poured it a saucer of milk,

shook her fist at it, smoked it in the chimney,

stamped on it, spanked it, dug a grave for it,

and she even — I am sorry to say —
spat at the night.

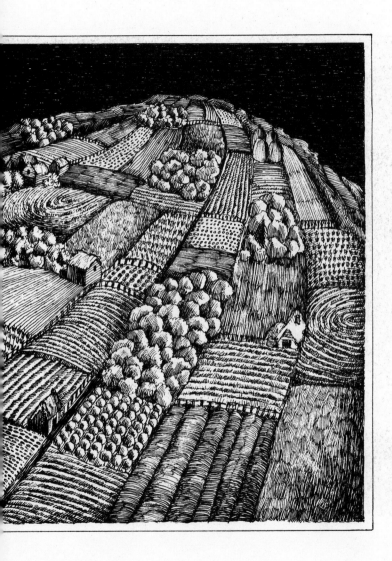

But the night took no notice.
"Then I shan't notice the night,"
sniffed old Hildilid,
and she turned her back on it.

At that moment the sun climbed over the hills of Hexham.
But Hildilid was too tired from fighting the night
to enjoy the day.

She settled down to sleep
in her straw bed
so she would be all fresh
and ready to turn her back
on the night
when it returned to Hexham...

Good Night